# The Countries

# Saudi Arabia

Bob Italia
**ABDO Publishing Company**

## visit us at
## www.abdopub.com

Published by ABDO Publishing Company, 4940 Viking Drive, Edina, Minnesota 55435.
Copyright © 2003 by Abdo Consulting Group, Inc. International copyrights reserved in all countries. No part of this book may be reproduced in any form without written permission from the publisher.

Printed in the United States.

Photo Credits: Corbis, AP/Wide World
Contributing Editors: Tamara L. Britton, Kristin Van Cleaf, Stephanie Hedlund
Art Direction & Maps: Neil Klinepier

### Library of Congress Cataloging-in-Publication Data

Italia, Bob, 1955-
   Saudi Arabia / Bob Italia.
     p. cm. -- (The countries)
   Includes index.
   Summary: Examines the history, geography, people, government, economy, art, and recreation of Saudi Arabia.
   ISBN 1-57765-840-X
    1. Saudi Arabia--Juvenile literature. [1. Saudi Arabia.] I. Title. II. Series.

  DS204.25 .I83 2002
  953.8--dc21

                                  2002018766

# Contents

# Ahalan!

Hello from Saudi Arabia!  People have lived in Saudi Arabia for thousands of years.  During this time, powerful families fought for control of the empire.  The Saud (sah-AHD) family finally gained control of the land.  In 1932, ibn Saud proclaimed it the Kingdom of Saudi Arabia.

Saudi Arabia's government is a monarchy.  The Council of Ministers advises the king on governmental issues. The Consultative Council also advises the king. But the king makes all decisions.

Saudi Arabians are a mix of many peoples.  Arabic is the country's official language.  Islam is its official religion.

Saudi Arabia has the largest **petroleum** reserves in the world.  Petroleum is the nation's main product. With money earned from selling oil, the government has built modern cities, new hospitals, and better schools.

Ahalan *from Saudi Arabia!*

# Fast Facts

**OFFICIAL NAME:** Kingdom of Saudi Arabia
**CAPITAL:** Riyadh

**LAND**
- Area: 756,999 square miles (1,960,626 sq km)
- Highest Peak: Jabal Sawda' 10,279 feet (3,133 m)
- Lowest Point: Persian Gulf (sea level)
- Deserts: An-Nafud, Ad-Dahna, Rub al-Khali

**PEOPLE**
- Population: 22,757,092 (July 2001 est.)
- Major Cities: Riyadh, Mecca, Medina
- Language: Arabic
- Religion: Islam

**GOVERNMENT**
- Form: Monarchy
- Head of State: King
- Legislature: None
- Flag: Green flag with white Arabic script in center. Beneath the script is a saber that points toward the mast side of the flag. The script says, "There is no God but God; Muhammad is the messenger of God."
- Independence: Kingdom declared September 23, 1932

**ECONOMY**
- Agricultural Products: Dates, wheat, barley, citrus; eggs, milk, chickens, cattle, goats, sheep
- Mining Products: Petroleum
- Money: Riyal (1 riyal = 100 halalahs)

*Saudi Arabia's flag*

*Saudi Arabian riyals*

# Timeline

| | |
|---|---|
| A.D. 570 | Muhammad is born |
| 632 | Muhammad dies |
| 1500 | Saud family controls much of Saudi Arabia |
| mid-1700s | Muhammad ibn Saud forms alliance with Muhammad ibn Abd al-Wahhab |
| 1806 | Saud family controls Saudi Arabia |
| 1891 | al-Rashid family captures Riyadh |
| 1902 | ibn Saud recaptures Riyadh |
| 1932 | ibn Saud proclaims Kingdom of Saudi Arabia |
| 1953 | Council of Ministers formed; Saud becomes king |
| 1958 | Saud names Faisal prime minister |
| 1960 | Saud regains power from Faisal |
| 1964 | Faisal becomes king |
| 1967 | Six Day War |
| 1973 | Yom Kippur War |
| 1975 | Faisal assassinated; Khalid becomes king |
| 1982 | Khalid dies; Fahd becomes king |
| 1990 | Iraq invades Kuwait |
| 1991 | Persian Gulf War |

# History

People have lived on the Arabian **Peninsula** for thousands of years. From the 400s B.C. to about A.D. 100, the Nabataeans controlled present-day Jordan and northwestern Saudi Arabia. The Sabaeans ruled the southern part of the peninsula, in what is now Yemen.

In about 570, Muhammad (moh-HAH-muhd) was born in Mecca. He brought Islam to the people. By the time he died in 632, Islam had spread throughout the land.

After Muhammad's death, his followers conquered the rest of the peninsula. Islam soon spread eastward into India. It eventually moved westward across North Africa into Spain.

During this time, powerful families fought for control of the land. In about 1500, the Saud family controlled much of the area. In the mid-1700s, Muhammad ibn

Saud formed an **alliance** with **fundamentalist** Islamic leader Muhammad ibn Abd al-Wahhab (wah-HAHB).

*King Abd al-Aziz ibn Saud (seated) with his son Saud*

During this time, many people wanted to practice a **strict** form of Islam. For this reason, the alliance between ibn Saud and al-Wahhab gave the Saud family a large following.

By 1806, the Saud family controlled Najd, Mecca, and Medina. The Saudis formed alliances with tribal leaders. They soon controlled most of the **peninsula's** east coast.

But in 1891, the rival al-Rashid (rah-SHEED) family captured the city of Riyadh (ree-YAHD). The Saud family fled to Kuwait. But in 1902, Abd al-Aziz ibn Saud recaptured Riyadh.

*King Saud*

During the next 25 years, ibn Saud expanded his empire. He regained all of the territory that his family had once controlled. In 1932, he proclaimed these lands the Kingdom of Saudi Arabia.

In 1953, ibn Saud organized the Council of Ministers to modernize the government. But later that year, he died. His oldest son Saud became king. Saud continued his father's government programs. But unwise government spending produced serious **economic** problems for Saudi Arabia.

In 1958, Saud appointed his brother Faisal (FI-suhl) **prime minister**. Faisal restored the economy. But he and Saud did not always agree on how to run the country. So in 1960, Saud resumed control of the government.

In the early 1960s, Saud became ill. In 1964, royal family members and religious leaders formed a council. They forced Saud to give up the throne, then made Faisal king.

In 1967, Faisal sent troops to Jordan and Syria to support Egypt in the Six Day War against Israel. Egypt had closed the Gulf of Aqaba (AH-kah-buh) to Israeli ships. For this reason, Israel had attacked Egypt.

Even with the help of many Arab countries, Egypt lost the war. After the war, Israel occupied the Sinai **Peninsula**, Syria's Golan Heights, and the Gaza Strip. Israel also controlled the area west of the Jordan River. This area, known as the West

*King Faisal*

Bank, was previously held by Jordan. It includes Jerusalem, one of Islam's holiest cities.

Arab governments were upset that Israel took this land. They called these areas occupied territories. The Saudi government said there would not be peace until Israel withdrew.

In 1973, Egypt and Syria, with the help of other Arab forces, attacked Israel. This attack started the Yom Kippur War. King Faisal decided to use **petroleum** as an **economic** weapon in the war. Saudi Arabia and

*An Israeli tank crew relaxes near their armored vehicle in Suez City during the Yom Kippur War.*

several other Arab countries stopped exporting
**petroleum** to nations that supported Israel. This
created worldwide fuel shortages.

The Arab countries still could not defeat Israel. But
lowering oil exports gave the Arab countries a

*King Khalid*

new-found power. And less oil in the world market meant higher prices. So many Arabs, including the Saud family, became very rich.

In March 1975, King Faisal was **assassinated**. His brother Prince Khalid (KAH-lid) became king and **prime minister**. Khalid died in 1982, and his brother Prince Fahd became king and prime minister.

In 1990, Iraqi forces invaded and occupied Kuwait. The Iraqis wanted Kuwait's oil. Saudi leaders feared Iraq would try to take their oil fields, too. A number of nations joined Saudi Arabia to liberate Kuwait.

The Persian Gulf War began in January 1991. The United States provided most of the troops and military equipment. Saudi Arabia provided the land base for the

*King Fahd*

*Crown Prince Abdullah*

attack. By the end of February, the allies had driven the Iraqis out of Kuwait.

In the late 1990s, King Fahd became ill. Since then, his brother Crown Prince Abdullah (ahb-duh-LAH) has helped run Saudi Arabia's government.

# A Desert Land

Saudi Arabia is located on the Arabian **Peninsula**. Its land is mostly desert, and has no rivers or lakes. Dry valleys called wadis can flood during rare rainstorms. But the water quickly **evaporates**, or soaks into the ground.

Saudi Arabia is divided into four land regions. They are the Najid, the Hejaz, the Asir, and the al-Hasa.

The Najid is the largest area. The city of Riyadh is here. Two great deserts are in this region, the An-Nafud and the Ad-Dahna.

The Hejaz is a long, narrow region. It runs along Saudi Arabia's border with the Red Sea. This coastal plain lies between the sea and the mountainous interior. The cities of Mecca and Medina are here.

North America
Europe
Asia
**DETAIL AREA**
Africa
South America
Australia
Antarctica

Lebanon
Syria
Iran
Israel
Iraq
United Arab Emirates
Jordan
Egypt
**Saudi Arabia**
PERSIAN GULF
Qatar
Oman
Eritrea
RED SEA
Yemen
Djibouti
Sudan
Somalia
Ethiopia
INDIAN OCEAN

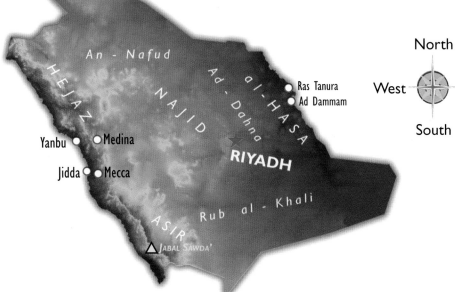

An - Nafud
HEJAZ
NAJID
Ad - Dahna
al - HASA
Ras Tanura
Ad Dammam
Yanbu
Medina
**RIYADH**
Jidda
Mecca
Rub al - Khali
ASIR
JABAL SAWDA'

North
West · East
South

The Asir is in the southwestern corner of Saudi Arabia. This area gets up to 12 inches (30 cm) of rain each year. This is more rain than falls anywhere else in the country.

The al-Hasa is in the east, along the Persian Gulf. This sandy area contains the country's rich oil reserves.

Southern Saudi Arabia, along the border with Yemen and Oman, is called the Rub al-Khali. This great desert is the largest continuous body of sand in the world.

*The Rub al-Khali*

# Rainfall

**Rain**

## AVERAGE YEARLY RAINFALL

| *Inches* | | *Centimeters* |
|---|---|---|
| Under 10 |  | Under 25 |
| 10 - 20 | | 25 - 50 |
| 20 - 59 | | 50 - 150 |

# Temperature

## AVERAGE TEMPERATURE

| *Fahrenheit* | | *Celsius* |
|---|---|---|
| Over 68° | 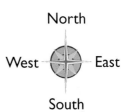 | Over 20° |
| 50° - 68° | | 10° - 20° |
| 32° - 50° | | 0° - 10° |

North
West — East
South

**Summer**

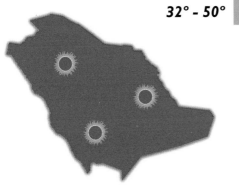

**Winter**

# Saudi Arabians

Saudi Arabians are a mix of many peoples. Their **culture** is a mixture of Arab, African, Indonesian, and Indian traditions.

Saudis are united by their religion. Islam is the country's official religion. The only non-Muslims in Saudi Arabia are foreigners.

Almost all Saudis speak Arabic. It is the official language of the country. Many Saudis also speak English. Students learn English in intermediate and secondary schools. It is also widely used in business.

The traditional family structure is important to the Saudis. Saudi fathers are the head of the family. Mothers have much authority in running the household. Outside the home, women have little freedom or opportunity for advancement.

Most Saudi families live in modern homes or high-rise buildings. People in the cities work in a variety of professions. Many have jobs in government, service, and industry. In rural areas, most Saudis live in farm villages or in **oases**.

*An urban Saudi Arabian family*

The Bedouins (BEH-duh-wuhnz) are desert **nomads** who live in large tents made of goat hair. They raise camels, goats, and sheep, and often move in search of water and pastureland.

*A man in a ghutra and an iqal holds his son.*

Seminomads move around much of the year, but spend several months in rural villages. A common village has a group of mud and stone houses, and a village marketplace. There, Saudis buy and sell goods and meet with friends. Today, many nomads and seminomads have settled on farms or in cities.

Most Saudis wear traditional Arabic clothes. An ankle-length cotton or wool garment called a *thawb* (THOBE) is popular with men. The *thawb* is often covered by a jacket or cloak. A *ghutra* (GOO-tra) is a cloth fastened over the head by a rope band called an *iqal* (EE-gal). It protects men from the sun and wind.

Women wear a full-length robe called an *abayah* (ah-BEE-yuh). When in public, most women cover their head with a scarf. They also cover their face with a veil.

*These women are wearing the traditional* abayah *and veil.*

The most popular foods in Saudi Arabia are dairy products, lamb, and rice. Dates, bread, fruits, and vegetables are a major part of the Saudi diet as well. Saudis can buy many imported and locally produced foods at supermarkets. Tea and coffee are the most popular drinks.

The government provides free education for its citizens. Attendance is not required by law. But more than 80 percent of children attend school. Almost equal numbers of boys and girls are enrolled in school.

*Today, many non-traditional foods are available in Saudi Arabia. These pilgrims are enjoying Kentucky Fried Chicken in a restaurant in Mecca.*

# Rangina

Rangina is a recipe that uses dates, one of Saudi Arabia's major crops.

- I pound fresh dates
- 1/2 cup butter
- 3/4 cup flour
- I teaspoon ground cardamom

Take the pits out of the dates and arrange them in six individual dessert dishes. Melt the butter in a heavy pan and stir in the flour. Cook until mixture is a golden-brown color. Remove pan from heat and stir in cardamom. Let the mixture cool, stirring occasionally. While it is still warm, pour mixture over the dates. Let cool to room temperature before serving. Serves six.

AN IMPORTANT NOTE TO THE CHEF: Always have an adult help with the preparation and cooking of food. Never use kitchen utensils or appliances without adult permission and supervision.

| English | Arabic |
|---------|--------|
| Yes | na'am (NAH-ahm) |
| No | laa (l-AH) |
| Thank you | shokran (SHUCK-rahn) |
| Please | min fadilak (mihn FAHD-lak) |
| Hello | ahalan (AH-lan) |
| Good-bye | ma'a el salama (mah el sah-LEH-mah) |

LANGUAGE

# The Government

Saudi Arabia's government is a monarchy. The Saud family rules the country. The king holds executive and legislative powers. He is also the country's spiritual leader.

The Council of Ministers advises the king on governmental issues. The king heads the Council and serves as **prime minister**. He has the power to appoint and dismiss the Council's members. He can also overrule all of their decisions.

Saudi Arabia also has a Consultative Council. It consists of a chairman and 90 other members. The members are appointed by the king. The Council gives the king advice but has no legislative authority.

The Basic Law of Government was issued in 1992. It made the **Koran** and **Sunna** the country's **constitution**.

The Koran and Sunna make up the ***Sharia***. It is the basis of Saudi law. Religious scholars known as *ulama* (oo-LAH-mah) interpret the *Sharia*. They make sure that Saudi Arabia's laws follow it.

*King Fahd arrives in Kuwait City to attend an Islamic summit meeting with leaders of other Islamic countries.*

# The Economy

Saudi Arabia has the largest **petroleum** reserves in the world. The country's oil fields hold about one-fourth of the world's oil. The Saudi Arabian Oil Company is owned by the state. It controls the Saudi Arabian oil industry.

Saudi Arabia is the world's largest exporter of petroleum. It is also a leading producer of natural gas. The country is a member of the Organization of Petroleum Exporting Countries.

Saudi Arabia has other valuable mineral resources. There are small deposits of gold in the Hejaz region. The land also contains clay, gypsum, limestone, and other minerals.

Mining and petroleum processing are the country's main sources of income. But most Saudis are farmers and herders. Only about one percent of Saudi Arabia's land is fertile. In this small area, farmers grow wheat, barley, fruits, dates, millet, sorghum, and tomatoes.

Herders keep cattle, goats, and sheep. These animals are important sources of dairy products and meat. Herders also raise chickens that produce eggs.

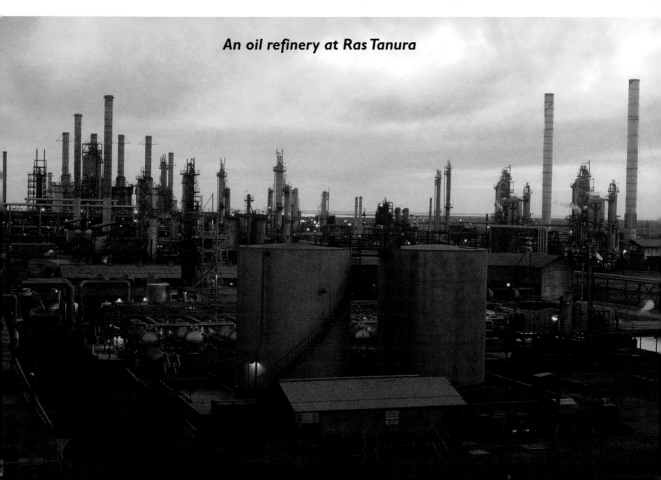

*An oil refinery at Ras Tanura*

# Beautiful Cities

Riyadh has been Saudi Arabia's capital since 1932. Riyadh has huge hotels and even larger hospitals. It also has one of the biggest airports in the world.

The center of Riyadh is called Al-Bathaa. This is the oldest part of the city. West of Al-Bathaa is the Riyadh Museum. It contains **artifacts** from the early days of Islam through today.

Southwest of Riyadh is the holy city of Mecca. Mecca is the birthplace of the Prophet

*Praying in Mecca*

Muhammad. Just north of Mecca is Medina. Here,
Muhammad established the first Islamic community.

Mecca and Medina are two of Islam's holy cities.
Every year, millions of Muslim **pilgrims** visit these
cities. They come from all over the world.

*Riyadh's skyline at dusk*

# From Here to There

Saudi Arabia has a wide system of roads. It connects the country's cities. The country has one railway. It runs between Riyadh and the Persian Gulf port of Ad Dammam.

Saudi Arabia's official airline is Saudi Arabian Airlines. It is owned and operated by the government. Ad Dammam, Dhahran, Jidda, and Riyadh have international airports.

The Persian Gulf port of Ras Tanura handles most of Saudi Arabia's oil exports. Another major Persian Gulf port is Ad Dammam. Jidda and Yanbu on the Red Sea are important, too.

*A Saudi Arabian Airlines plane*

*Saudi cameleers*

# Holidays & Festivals

Saudi Arabian **culture** revolves almost entirely around Islam. Most of Saudi Arabia's holidays are Islamic.

Ramadan is the major Islamic holiday. Ramadan lasts for a month. During this time, people can't eat, drink, or smoke between sunrise and sunset.

The end of Ramadan marks another major holiday. It is called Eid al-Fitr. During Eid al-Fitr, Saudis pray, visit friends, give presents, and have a big feast.

Eid al-Adah is the other big feast of the year. It is held around March. This holiday marks the time when Muslims make the annual **pilgrimage** to Mecca.

There is only one non-religious festival in Saudi Arabia. It is the Jinadriyah National Festival. This festival is held every February.

One of Saudi Arabia's most popular folk rituals is the *Ardha* (ahrd-HAH). This is the country's national dance. It is based on ancient Bedouin traditions.

*Muslim women on pilgrimage to Mecca*

In the *Ardha*, drummers beat out a rhythm. A poet chants verses to the drumbeat. And men dance shoulder to shoulder, while carrying swords.

# Sports & Leisure

In Saudi Arabia, socializing is the most popular form of entertainment. Since public movie theaters are not allowed, many Saudis turn to radios, televisions, and home videos for entertainment.

Saudi men enjoy playing modern sports such as basketball, soccer, and volleyball. Traditional sports, such as camel and horse racing, are also popular.

In many areas, the village marketplace acts as a social center. While buying and selling goods, Saudis chat with friends.

*Opposite page: Lee Young Pyo (R) of South Korea tries to get the ball from Saudi Arabia's Talal al-Meshal (L) in the Asian Cup 2000 semifinal game. The Saudi Arabian team won the game 2 to 1.*

# Glossary

**alliance** - people, groups, or nations joined for a common cause.

**artifact** - anything made by human skill or work a long time ago.

**assassinate** - to murder an important or famous person, usually for political reasons.

**constitution** - the laws that govern a country.

**culture** - the customs, arts, and tools of a people or nation at a certain time.

**economy** - the way a nation uses its money, goods, and natural resources.

**evaporate** - to change from liquid or solid into vapor.

**fundamentalist** - a person who supports strict devotion to a set of principles.

**Koran** - the sacred book of Islam. It contains Islam's religious and moral code. Muslims believe the Koran is the word of Allah, as revealed by the archangel Gabriel to the Prophet Muhammad.

**nomad** - a member of a tribe that moves from place to place in search of food or pasture for its animals. Seminomads move from place to place part of the year, and stay in one place the rest of the year.

**oasis** - a place in the desert with water, trees, and plants.

**peninsula** - land that sticks out into water and is connected to a larger land mass.

**petroleum** - a thick, yellowish-black oil. It is the source of gasoline.

**pilgrimage** - a journey to a holy place. A person on a pilgrimage is called a pilgrim.

**prime minister** - the highest-ranking member of some governments.

**Sharia** - a complete legal system that governs all aspects of a Muslim's life. It is derived directly from the Koran and the teachings of the Prophet Muhammad.

**strict** - severely conforming to a principle or condition.

**Sunna** - the body of Islamic custom and practice based on the Prophet Muhammad's words and deeds.

# Web Sites

Would you like to learn more about Saudi Arabia? Please visit **www.abdopub.com** to find up-to-date Web site links about the country's government and people. These links are routinely monitored and updated to provide the most current information available.

# Index